# GOOD WORDS

# good words

## INSPIRATION FOR CATHOLIC WOMEN

ST. ANTHONY MESSENGER PRESS
Cincinnati, Ohio

Edited by Mary Curran-Hackett
Cover and book design by Mark Sullivan
Cover image © istockphoto.com | Donald Erickson

LIBRARY OF CONGRESS CATALOGING-IN-PUBLICATION DATA
Good words : inspiration for Catholic women / [edited by Mary Curran-Hackett].
        p. cm.
Includes bibliographical references (p.        ).
ISBN 978-0-86716-956-0 (alk. paper)
1. Catholic women—Prayers and devotions. I. Curran-Hackett, Mary.
BX2170.W7G66 2010
242'.62—dc22
                                        2010031270
ISBN 978-0-86716-956-0

Published by St. Anthony Messenger Press
28 W. Liberty St.
Cincinnati, OH 45202
www.AmericanCatholic.org
www.SAMPBooks.org

Printed in the United States of America.
Printed on acid-free paper.

10 11 12 13 14   5 4 3 2 1

# Contents

· · · · ·

Introduction: For Everything There Is a Season,
and a Few Good Words : ix

For Every Matter Under Heaven : 1

A Time to Be Born : 8

A Time to Die : 15

A Time to Plant, A Time to Pluck Up What Is Planted : 22

A Time to Kill, A Time to Heal : 29

A Time to Break Down, A Time to Build Up : 37

A Time to Weep, A Time to Laugh : 45

A Time to Mourn, A Time to Dance : 54

A Time to Throw Away Stones, A Time to Gather Stones Together : 63

A Time to Embrace, A Time to Refrain From Embracing : 71

A Time to Seek, and a Time to Lose : 80

A Time to Keep, A Time to Throw Away : 87

A Time to Tear, A Time to Sew : 96

A Time to Keep Silence, A Time to Speak : 103

A Time to Love, A Time to Hate : 110

A Time for War, A Time for Peace : 119

Notes : 127

*v*

. . . . .

For everything there is a season,
and a time for every matter under heaven:
a time to be born, and a time to die;
a time to plant, and a time to pluck up what is planted;
a time to kill, and a time to heal;
a time to break down, and a time to build up;
a time to weep, and a time to laugh;
a time to mourn, and a time to dance;
a time to throw away stones, and a time to gather stones together;
a time to embrace, and a time to refrain from embracing;
a time to seek, and a time to lose;
a time to keep, and a time to throw away;
a time to tear, and a time to sew;
time to keep silence, and a time to speak;
a time to love, and a time to hate;
a time for war, and a time for peace.

—Ecclesiastes 3:1–8

. . . . .

# *Introduction*

## For Everything There Is a Season, and a Few Good Words

Good words inspire us in times of hope, grief, despair, joy, love, hate, pain, war, and peace. Good words affirm our gifts and talents during happy times and they encourage us in the depths of our despair. Good words help us persevere no matter what obstacles come our way, and comfort us when life's circumstances seem beyond our comprehension or ability to cope. Good words provide healing to the pain our mortal bodies endure. Moreover, they show us what our indefatigable and immortal souls can overcome. Good words provoke thought and, in time, even change, no matter what time, season, or period of life.

The excerpts and quotations—or rather, the good words—that appear in this book all come from published works from this press. The collected wisdom of the St. Anthony Messenger Press authors in *Good Words* is intended to be a companion in the quiet (and perhaps even the not-so-quiet) moments of your day. Whether you are just waking, on your way to a meeting, waiting for someone to arrive, or just about to go to bed, you'll find a brief reflection and line of Scripture, along with excerpts from various St. Anthony Messenger Press books, as well as questions to reflect upon no matter what time of day or time in your life.

May these good words inspire you—today, tomorrow, and in every time and season and matter under heaven—throughout your life as a Catholic woman.

..... 

*For Every Matter Under Heaven*

.....

So God created humankind in his image,
in the image of God he created them;
male and female he created them.
(Genesis 1:27)

**Reflection**
*From the beginning God had a plan for all of creation. God created us with hope, love, life, and spirit. Each one of us has a purpose, and each one of us is created by God to fulfill this purpose while on earth—all in the hope that one day we will rejoice with God in heaven.*

. . . . .

*Good Words*

. . . . .

## Why Am I Here?

Does God have a plan for my life? None of us can really know the answer to that question, but God promises not to abandon us in our pursuit. God is not going to leave us to our own defenses. God will put people and situations and opportunities in our path. God gives us everything we need to choose what is good. Discovering God's dream for our life can be scary. There is undue pressure to find the one right thing, but any decision we make is never the last decision. It is just the next decision. I don't have to worry about forever, if I am able to concentrate on doing the next right thing. Perhaps finding our vocation means making the best decision given everything I know up to this point.

—Beth M. Knobbe, *Finding My Voice: A Young Woman's Perspective*

## Questions for Reflection

*"Why am I here?" It's the most fundamental question, and yet how much time do you devote to thinking or praying about God's purpose for you? What do you think God expects from you? What can you do—today—to take a step closer to God and what God hopes for you?*

### Taking the Risk

I don't have to know everything the future holds, but fidelity requires that we remain in the conversation. Finding our calling requires risk. Our calling might look different from what we first expected. Discernment entails gathering information, using our imagination and sense of humor, engaging in conversation, and asking a lot of questions. It takes patience and prayer, and perhaps a good mentor or spiritual guide. We need to be open, willing, and able to move in whatever direction the Spirit calls us.

—Beth M. Knobbe, *Finding My Voice: A Young Woman's Perspective*

### Questions For Reflection

*What do you think the future holds for you? What risks are you willing to take to make your future happen?*

## Finding God in Others and Ourselves

We are immersed in relationships and if we desire to follow the path of Jesus we have to develop the capacity to see God in ourselves and others—*all* others, at *all* times. Developing this capacity requires that we trust that the Word within is contained in each person, circumstance or relationship with which we are involved. An even greater challenge is to remain convinced of this when that is not immediately apparent. Responding and relating to the deeper truth, regardless of what a given situation presents, opens the door to manifesting the Christ consciousness in ourselves and calling it forth in others.

—Mary H. Reaman, *Wake Up to God's Word: Exercises
for Spiritual Transformation*

## Questions for Reflection

*Do you see Christ's image in everyone you meet? Your friends? Your enemies?*

*Think of someone you consider an enemy or someone who simply tries your patience. Find a quality of Christ in that person. Pray for this person today. And every time you see him or her try to focus on the image of Christ within. Does it change the way you see or treat this person?*

## Changing Our Imaginings of the God Before Us

If our relationship with God has not changed over the years, if we are still praying in the same way we prayed as children—or if we have quit praying altogether—if our image of God is still an old man with a white beard, we can be sure that our relationship with God has grown stale and stagnant.

—Mary H. Reaman, *Wake Up to God's Word: Exercises for Spiritual Transformation*

## Questions for Reflection

*What do you imagine God to look like today? What do you do to nurture your relationship with God?*

## Spiritual, But Not Religious

Religion and spirituality are not separate entities. On the contrary, religion and spirituality are integrally linked. Spirituality is more than achieving stillness of mind, quietness of heart, or a balanced life. Religion is more than blind acceptance of doctrine or rigid adherence to rules. Religious practices give voice to spirituality, and spirituality gives meaning to our rites and rituals. Spirituality without religion is empty belief, and religion without spirituality is uninspiring....

To be both spiritual and religious is to recognize that all of life exists in relationship to God. Instead of compartmentalizing our life, we see all of life as one contiguous plane where our work, personal relationships, family and social activities are not separate but essential to the spiritual life.

—Beth M. Knobbe, *Finding My Voice: A Young Woman's Perspective.*

## Questions for Reflection

*Do you consider yourself spiritual, but not religious? Why? What practices make you feel more spiritual?*

## United in Humanity, in God

We are called to be united in the one God of love and will find no rest in the universe until we rest in this love. Christ is the way, the truth and the life and if we are unsure of the way to travel then we have only to look and see the God who is bent over in love for us. We must bend down to see God. We will find him there in the frailty of our humanity, among the poor, the sick, the lame and the blind. Yes, God is there and will always be there until the end of time. For our God is a humble God and faithful in love. He simply needs flesh and blood and a human face to show his goodness. God needs human skin to live in the universe, vessels of passionate love. We have the capacity for God; we are made in God's image. We can be and are called to be co-lovers and co-creators of the universe. We are called to be alive in Christ, the Living One, in whom dwells the promise and future of God.

—Ilia Delio, O.S.F., *The Humility of God: A Franciscan Perspective*

## Questions for Reflection

*When do you see God's goodness in your life? How do you "bend" down to see God? Do you help with the sick, the poor? Do you see God when you care for or look at children?*

· · · · ·
*A Time to Be Born*
· · · · ·

"And she gave birth to her firstborn son
and wrapped him in bands of cloth,
and laid him in the manger,
because there was no place
for them in the inn."
(Luke 2:7)

### Reflection

*There are few certainties that unite all of humanity, but there are two irrefutable facts we can all agree on: We are all born of a mother and we all die. God sent us his Son, Jesus, through Mary to share in this humanity, this gift of life. Whenever a child is born or we begin anew, we are reminded of this special gift and our role in God's plan.*

. . . . .
## *Good Words*
. . . . .

**Yes to New Life**

It's a defining moment for Mary: Will she embrace what the angel is saying? Will she accept this incredible idea that she will be the Mother of God? Will she beat back her doubt and agree to walk this path, a path that will lead to goodness knows where?

She does. Somehow, this young girl looks at the incomprehensible future offered to her, makes herself larger than her fear, and says: I'll take it.

—Ginny Kubitz Moyer, *Mary and Me: Catholic Women Reflect on the Mother of God*

**Questions for Reflection**

*What doubts do you have about the choices you're making in your life today? What is holding you back from saying "yes" to opportunities for growth and new life?*

## Embracing the Unknown

…[A]nother reason why the Annunciation is so compelling to women today is because every one of us can, on some level, relate to Mary's moment of decision. Though she's the only one in history who has been offered the chance to become the Mother of God, the process of navigating our way through life's choices is universal to humankind. Like Mary, every one of us has had the experience of being at a turning point in life, pondering the options that lie before us.

—Ginny Kubitz Moyer, *Mary and Me: Catholic Women Reflect on the Mother of God*

## Questions for Reflection

*One of the most wonderful and terrifying aspects of giving birth—is the unknown. No one knows what will be. How do you embrace the unknown? Have you ever experienced a time when you said yes to the unknown, and discovered yourself in the process? What things about yourself did you discover?*

## Giving Birth to Love and Justice

A firm intention aligns us with the labor of God in God's birthing of love and justice. God does this birthing repeatedly; we can participate and be changed in the process. People sometimes mock intention —the way to hell is paved with good ones; however, it makes all the difference in the world. Intention indicates a conscious choice to give it my best shot—on this day or in this hour at work, with my child, in a difficult relationship.

—Clare Wagner, *Awakening to Prayer: A Woman's Perspective*

## Questions for Reflection

*What conscious choices do you make every day that give birth to God's justice in the world? How can you live a life with more intention?*

## Transforming With Intention

Intention makes us conscious of a direction we choose to take. Giving voice to concrete intention is a way to make ourselves conscious that, with God's companionship, we can transform ordinary activities into sacred moments:

- I intend to live this day aware of God's presence within and around me.
- I intend to make healthy choices for my body, mind, and spirit today.
- I intend to look for the Divine spark in every human face I see today.
- I intend to notice beauty in some piece of nature today.
- I intend to hold, with God's strength and love, the wounded world in my heart.

—Clare Wagner, *Awakening to Prayer: A Woman's Perspective*

## Questions for Reflection

*Pick one intention and practice it all day. Before you go to sleep, ask yourself how it made difference in your day. Were you transformed?*

## What Could I Say?

How could I explain to them that when you first hold that baby that weighs under ten pounds, you realize the weight of the world now rests in your arms?

How can I tell them that when you first lay eyes on your child, you are not counting fingers and toes, but you are counting indescribable blessings?

How can you explain that the thing your heart does when it feels like it will absolutely burst out of the confines of your chest?

And how can you explain to any parents-to-be that the next few days will be filled with tears? Tears of joy, tears of frustration, and sometimes tears for reasons only a parent's heart can understand.

—Tammy Bundy, *The Book of Mom: What Parents Know By Heart*

## Questions for Reflection

*Think of the parents—birth, adoptive, foster, or parent-like individuals—in your life. Do you ever think of the day they first saw you? Can you imagine the love and joy they felt and showered upon you? Remember this love and joy always, and when you see or pray for your parents, remember to offer your gratitude for the gift of life.*

## Birth and Death

On the ninth floor were two parents who were waiting to hold their miracle for which they had been waiting for years. They were waiting and praying to bring their son into this world. And on the sixth floor, there waited two parents who were also waiting for a miracle. They were waiting and praying to keep their son in this world.

In the big script of life we never know what ironies will touch us along the way. Some will bring a laugh of complete joy. Others will bring a tear of utter sorrow.

So many times we wish we could simply flip ahead in the script to see what scenes are coming.

But we can't.

All we can do is take a deep breath.

Turn one page at a time.

And pray.

—Tammy Bundy, *The Book of Mom: What Parents Know By Heart*

## Questions for Reflection

*There is nothing that makes us appreciate life as much as witnessing the birth of a miracle or realizing the imminence of death. Have you ever experienced the birth and death of loved ones at the same time? How did it affect or change how you experienced your life?*

## A Time to Die

…"The Son of Man must undergo great suffering,
and be rejected by the elders, chief priests, and scribes,
and be killed, and on the third day be raised."
Then he said to them all, "If any want to become my followers,
let them deny themselves and take up their cross daily and
follow me. For those who want to save their life will lose it,
and those who lose their life for my sake will save it."
(Luke 9:22–24)

**Reflection**
*No one born to this life escapes it without experiencing suffering, loss, and death. It is this suffering that unites all of humanity together and unites all of humanity with Jesus Christ. Jesus died with us and for us, and because he did this we can face our own suffering (and that of our loved ones) and ultimately our own death with courage, dignity, and love. And it is because of this knowledge of death that we can live our lives more fully, more intentioned, and more hopeful than without it. And thanks to Jesus Christ's death and resurrection, we know that when we die with him and for him, we are all born again—into eternal life.*

. . . . .
# *Good Words*
. . . . .

## When Death Knocks on Our Door

In all cases we experience some shift in consciousness, some change in the way we see the world, ourselves and God. This the point at which an authentic change of direction may begin, a change for the better, what Christians refer to as *conversion*.

—Dolores R. Leckey, *Grieving With Grace: A Woman's Perspective*

## Questions for Reflection

*Have you lost someone close to you? Who? Reflect on this person's life and death. How did his or her life affect you? How did his or her death convert you?*

*Think of your own death. How do you want to be remembered? What changes do you hope your life and death inspire in your loved ones?*

## There Are Many Ways to Be Dead

We can be dead in any number of ways, long before the body dies. We can be intellectually dead, not letting in new ideas or new possibilities. We can be emotionally dead, letting love dry up. We can even be physically dead while still breathing, alienated from our bodies and our sexuality. All of these aspects of our being desperately need the new of resurrection, and the way that resurrection happens will surely rise from our everyday lives and may not always be immediately recognizable.

—Dolores R. Leckey, *Grieving With Grace: A Woman's Perspective*

## Questions for Reflection

*What areas of your life are dead right now? What areas can you resurrect?*

*Are you still learning new things and opening yourself up to new experiences and possibilities? What new things are you willing to try?*

## A Chance to Start Over

Each day, a new beginning. A day to have wounds healed. A day to believe. A day to welcome home parts of ourselves that we have refused to embrace. These words about beginnings…are special comfort to me when I lose my temper, talk too much, and hurt people's feelings, act compulsively, or succumb to deep, deep laziness of mind, body and spirit.

— Lyn Holley Doucet, *Healing Troubled Hearts: Daily Spiritual Exercises*

## Questions for Reflection

*Every new beginning comes out of an ending—a death of sorts. What parts of you are you willing to let die so that better parts can be born or take their rightful place in your life?*

*What are the best parts of yourself that you have let die because you have refused to embrace them?*

## Learning From Those Who Have Suffered and Died Before Us

It is not surprising then that the mystics and saints of Christian spirituality almost always experienced illness at some point in their lives. Ignatius of Loyola's conversion occurred while he was recuperating from a serious leg wound. Julian of Norwich's visions of Jesus came while she was thought to be dying. Thérèse of Lisieux suffered agonies while dying of tuberculosis at the tender age of twenty-four, yet she exhibited the radical trust in God that was so vital to her spirituality. Indeed, it is difficult to find a saint or a mystic whose life has *not* been touched significantly by disability or illness.

—Janice McGraine, S.S.J., *Saints to Lean On:*
*Spiritual Companions for Illness and Disability*

## Questions for Reflection

*What can you learn from the lives of people who suffer from illness or disability?*

*If you suffer from chronic illness or disability, does it comfort you to know others have suffered before you or suffer with you?*

## Humor, Even in Death

Among the saints whose witness assures me that holy laughter is as necessary on the deathbed as clean sheets is Thérèse of Lisieux. During her long and painful bout with tuberculosis, the young Carmelite occasionally unsheathed the sword of ironic humor. When Thérèse once refused a cup of broth offered by a sister Carmelite, the nun stomped off in a snit, complaining that Thérèse could not possibly be the saint she was rumored to be because she was not even a good religious. To this insult, Thérèse replied, "What a benefaction to hear on one's deathbed that one has not even been a proper nun."

—Gloria Hutchinson, *Be Comforted: Healing in Times of Loss*

## Questions for Reflection

*While death is terrible, it does not have to be unbearable. How can you help someone dying forget their pain and suffering for a moment? Have you tried humor? Offered a joke? Watched a funny movie together? Recalled a fond memory together?*

*How do you feel about death? Do you think there is a place for humor or self-deprecation during this time?*

## Know This About Death

Know for certain that death does not end my relationships with all those I love. We will go on loving each other beyond time and telling.

—Gloria Hutchinson, *Be Comforted: Healing in Times of Loss*

## Questions for Reflection

*Who do you fear losing most in your life? Are you comforted by this knowledge—that you will be able to go on loving each other "beyond time and telling"?*

*Think of someone you have lost to this world. How has your love or relationship changed, endured? What do you miss most about this person? How did you learn to live without him or her? What was the most difficult adjustment?*

## A Time to Plant, A Time to Pluck Up What Is Planted

. . . . .

Do not be deceived; God is not mocked, for you reap whatever you
sow. If you sow to your own flesh, you will reap corruption from
the flesh; but if you sow to the Spirit, you will reap eternal life
from the Spirit. So let us not grow weary in doing what is right,
for we will reap at harvest time, if we do not give up. So then,
whenever we have an opportunity, let us work for the good of
all, and especially for those of the family of faith.
(Galatians 6:7–10)

### Reflection
*The Bible is full of gardening references. God's people are often referred to as
gardeners or the seeds themselves. We also reap what we sow. When we are
planted in rich soil we grow into large, abundant trees. We're also grains of
wheat gathered in barns after the weeds have been burned. We are watered.
We are shined upon. We grow. We bring beauty to the world. We plant
and we pluck. There is a time and a season for both. God is our Supreme
Gardener and we his beautiful flowers. Bloom on!*

. . . . .

*Good Words*

. . . . .

## What Talents Are "Seeded" Within You?

Talents offer a gateway into full participation within the kingdom of God, here and now. Faithful development and use of the talents seeded within ourselves allows contribution and participation in creating abundant life for the world. We have spent time praying with the things that bring us joy and the passion and actions that make us come alive! God does not give us talents for our own pleasure and purpose, rather God gives us talents primarily to serve the world in simple and generous ways.

—Pegge Bernecker, *Your Spiritual Garden: Tending to the Presence of God*

## Questions for Reflection

*What talents do you possess? Which one stands out as your best talent?*

*Do you use this talent every day? If not, why not? What can you do today to start doing so?*

## Growing With Your Talents

As talents grow and shift throughout our life, so do the ways we use our talents. Like the servant in the Scripture… [Matthew 25:20–23], we learn that eventually greater responsibility and joy come through the cultivation of our gifts.

—Pegge Bernecker, *Your Spiritual Garden: Tending to the Presence of God*

## Questions for Reflection

*What new talents have you discovered with age? How do they express the person you are today?*

*Have you experienced "greater responsibility and joy" through the discovery and growth of new talents? How so? If not, what do you think you can do to feel this joy?*

## Outgrowing Talents

We have the choice to exercise talents or allow them to wither and die. Similar to a garden in bloom, our talents can flourish and then outgrow the places we allow them to occupy. We must not be fearful to seek the new and unknown horizon where our talents can be magnified and expanded.

—Pegge Bernecker, *Your Spiritual Garden: Tending to the Presence of God*

## Questions for Reflection

*What talents have you excelled at? And what talents have outgrown the places they occupy? Are you exceptional at your job, but afraid to leave its security in order to seek out an "unknown horizon"? Do you possess an amazing talent, which lies outside your comfort zone, so much so, you're afraid of trying and perhaps failing?*

*What activity can you begin today to help an exceptional talent bloom and reach its full potential?*

## Not Just Being Followers of Christ

I'm not a gardener or writer, but I am a mother. My children are a part of who I am. Their needs are my needs. I think being a Christian means feeling that way about everyone, friend and foe. Taking care of others' needs as deftly as we take care of our children's or own should be a natural response, and not done just because it is the rule. When that happens, we are not just followers of Christ; we are Christ.

—Judith Dunlap, *Bringing Home the Gospel: The Year of Matthew*

## Questions for Reflections

*Whether you are a gardener, a writer, a mother, a doctor, a lawyer, a teacher, you are called to be your best at whatever it is you are doing. Do you put your entire heart and soul into everything you do? Is it a duty, an obligation, or a natural response?*

*What ways do you tend to others' needs? To your own?*

## Nurturing Your Relationship With God

Our relationship with God is like any other relationship. If we open ourselves and allow ourselves to be exposed to the presence and power of God, we will be changed by it. Our relationship with God has to be nurtured so that as we grow, it grows, as we change it changes and as it blossoms, we blossom into the person we are called to be.

—Mary Reaman, *Wake Up to God's Word:*
*Exercises for Spiritual Transformation*

## Questions for Reflection

*In your garden of friendships, which ones need more pruning, attention, or light? Which ones need to be weeded out because they have become toxic or damaging?*

*What is your relationship like with God today? Have you nourished it with prayer? Time together? Gratitude and appreciation? If so, how has your relationship with God grown over the years? If you haven't, in what ways do you feel most disconnected?*

## Tending to Our Spiritual Practices

Our spiritual practice will only bear fruit if we put our relationship with God first. Prayer and contemplation are the portals through which communication flows, intimacy grows and a sense of the interconnectedness of all things arises, but putting our relationship with God first demands that we return time and time again to such practices—whether or not we are able to discern the fruit of our labors.

—Mary Reaman, *Wake Up to God's Word:*
*Exercises for Spiritual Transformation*

## Questions for Reflection

*Do you put your relationship with God first? What things are getting in the way of your relationship with God today?*

*How often do you pray? Could you find a bit more time in your day to sit and talk with God?*

## A Time to Kill, A Time to Heal

. . . . .

The LORD kills and brings to life;
he brings down to Sheol and raises up.
The LORD makes poor and makes rich;
he brings low, he also exalts.
He raises up the poor from the dust;
he lifts the needy from the ash heap,
to make them sit with princes
and inherit a seat of honor.

(1 Samuel 2:6–8)

When the crowds found out about it, they followed him; and he
welcomed them, and spoke to them about the kingdom of God,
and healed those who needed to be cured.

(Luke 9:11)

**Reflection**

*The Old Testament promised us a Savior that would bring us new life—
heal us, exalt us, and raise us up. The New Testament shared with us how
Jesus fulfilled these prophecies over and over again. There are over a 120*

mentions of the word heal in the Bible—and for good reason. With Jesus' life we are given hope and healing to the death, destruction, and suffering that exists in the world. In Christ's healing, he kills the death and suffering of our old life and brings us a new, eternal life. In our own healing, we can bring new life and spirit to all those who need it.

. . . . .
## *Good Words*
. . . . .

### Jesus as the Crucified Christ

The *Via Crucis* (Way of the Cross) is a central dimension of Latina devotion to the crucified Christ. While this solemn Good Friday ritual may seem to the outsider like merely a drama, play, or simple reenactment, it is not. Through the reenactment of Jesus' death, the community is reliving Jesus' suffering, torture, and crucifixion. It is happening in the here and now. On this day, the community accompanies Jesus, just as he has accompanied them through their struggles and trials.

—Michelle A. Gonzalez, *Embracing Latina Spirituality: A Woman's Perspective*

### Questions for Reflection

*How do you view the Good Friday Way of the Cross? Is it simply a drama or reenactment for you? Or do you feel Christ's pain, his agony, and his suffering as if it were your own?*

*How might contemplating Christ's death help you through your own struggles?*

## Jesus as Healer

We have looked…at Jesus as he actively healed and converted those he walked with so many years ago. We believe that he desires in the same way to heal and to be with us. I hope you have embraced in a new and deeper way the image of Jesus as healer. His was a heart filled with compassion for the suffering he saw around him. His was a heart that reached out to the little ones and still reaches out to all that is little within us. I hope that in your life you will visit the healing miracles of the Bible often and embrace them for yourself.

—Lyn Holley Doucet, *Healing Troubled Hearts: Daily Spiritual Exercises*

## Questions for Reflection

*Do you find it difficult to believe in miraculous healings? If you do doubt their occurrence, why? What makes it hard for you to believe these things are possible even today?*

*Think of Jesus as your own healer. If he could heal you of one ailment—spiritual or physical—what would it be? Pray for that healing today.*

## Suffering That Brings Change

Each of us can pray for, and expect to notice, the tremendous woundedness in the world; experience a broken heart in the face of such suffering; and allow this suffering to awaken in us a desire for change. Since the journey will be difficult, we know we can't walk this path alone. Sensing this truth is a sign of readiness for the transformational journey. It signals that "your salvation is at hand." God's longing for you and your thirst for God converge, and you are gifted with the courage to take steps on the spiritual path that you and God will cocreate. The call isn't always as clear as what I have just described.

—Clare Wagner, *Awakening to Prayer: A Woman's Perspective*

## Questions for Reflection

*How has suffering changed you?*

*What types of "tremendous woundedness" are you aware of in the world? What can you do about any of it? How do you attempt to heal?*

## Opening Up to Healing and Change

I open myself to healing grace.

I ask for freedom from fear.

I long for your loving energy, my God, to fill my whole being.

Help me to believe that nothing can separate me from you.

Give me the grace, please, to look beyond my own needs and
wants.

O Sacred Presence, show me the way.

—Clare Wagner, *Awakening to Prayer: A Woman's Perspective*

## Questions for Reflection

*Are you open to God's healing grace? Is there any part of you that is afraid of being healed, because you are afraid of the changes that healing might bring?*

*What positive steps can you take today to begin to heal yourself—spiritually and physically? Do one thing today to move yourself in the direction of healing.*

## Healing in the Ordinary Actions of Life

Remember the resurrected Jesus? He was recognized in the ordinary actions of life: preparing food on the beach, eating with friends, walking and conversing with friends.

—Dolores R. Leckey, *Grieving With Grace: A Woman's Perspective*

## Questions for Reflection

*Think of all your activities during the day—talking with friends, neighbors, or coworkers, sitting alone in your car listening to your favorite song, or hugging your children or spouse. Which ones bring you the most joy and let you forget your troubles? How can you find more time for moments like these, which bring healing and connection in your daily life?*

*Now think of all the activities that sap your energy or make you angry or distressed. Perhaps talking to a negative friend or coworker, or listening to an abrasive radio personality? What can you do today to change your routine to "kill" such interactions, so that healing is possible? What can you do to better tolerate or control your reaction to these situations?*

## Everyone Deserves Healing and Love

Mother [Teresa's] love for life was an uncut quilt. She taught me to love life wherever I found it, in an unborn child, a person with Hansen's disease, a condemned murderer, someone with AIDS, someone taking his last breath. She often ended her talks with, "It's not how much we do, it's how much love we put into it."

—Maryanne Raphael, *What Mother Teresa Taught Me*

## Questions for Reflection

*How much love do you put into your daily activities? If you find you are doing things out of responsibility or obligation instead of love, do you find yourself feeling resentful, unappreciated, and entitled (that people owe you something for your work)? How can you change your attitude today about these obligations? How can you do them with more love? When your day is over, consider how differently you feel after doing these acts selflessly.*

## A Time to Break Down, A Time to Build Up

. . . . .

But this is how you must deal with them:
break down their altars, smash their pillars,
hew down their sacred poles,
and burn their idols with fire.
(Deuteronomy 7:5)

It shall be said,
"Build up, build up, prepare the way,
remove every obstruction from my people's way."
(Isaiah 57:14)

### Reflection

*The Old Testament speaks of tearing down and building up quite a bit. The two have always gone hand-in-hand. One can't build anew without tearing down the old. The New Testament echoes this message, but focuses especially on the notion of building up—not just buildings and traditions—but the individual as well. In the First Letter to the Thessalonians, we hear Paul say, "Therefore encourage one another and build up each other, as indeed you are doing" (5:11).*

37

. . . . .
## Good Words
. . . . .

### Build Yourself Up

Sometimes in the dream of making a difference in the world, our number one enemy is ourselves. We sabotage our dreams, thinking we are too young, too old, too skilled, too unskilled, too poor or too out of it. The truth is that change in the world is effected by people with strengths and weaknesses. Change is effected by ordinary people, and most of us are simply that—ordinary.

—Joan Mueller, *Living a Spirituality of Action: A Woman's Perspective*

### Questions for Reflection

*In what ways do you tear yourself down? Why do you think you're so hard on yourself?*

*In what ways have you sabotaged your life or relationships? What negative aspects of your personality have you refused to address? How do they cause you to make the same self-defeating mistakes?*

## Being Rather Than Doing

God has a much better plan for us than working and suffering all our lives. "Doing" does not equal worthiness or holiness. God does not expect us to spend this life working to the point of exhaustion and putting relationships and creativity aside in favor of getting just one more task done. God has other dreams for us.

—Susan K. Rowland, *Make Room for God: Clearing Out the Clutter*

## Questions for Reflection

*People often measure success and accomplishments in life by the hours they spent in the office that day, how many dollars they have in their bank accounts, or how many new electronics they have stashed in their designer purses, but God doesn't measure our success and our worthiness by such things. How do you measure your worth? What do you value?*

*What is God's dream for you? What is your dream? Is your daily list of tasks getting you closer to achieving your dream or is it taking you further away?*

## Overdoing a Good Thing

Clare's mortifications can only be understood in terms of her ardent love for God and the matching desire to express it in heroic fashion. Both Clare and Francis will realize too late, when their health begins to fail, that they have overdone a good thing.

—Joanne Turpin, *Women in Church History: 21 Stories for 21 Centuries*

## Questions for Reflection

*What parts of yourself are you willing to destroy or tear down, in order to build a new and better version of yourself?*

*Have you ever overdone a good thing? Have you fasted too long, denied yourself too much? What happened? How did it make you feel? Did you realize at some point the denial had less to do with what God wanted, and more to do with your own desires or pride?*

## Rebuilding Familiar Relationships

Even if we've managed to adjust to being adults in the presence of our mothers, we will always be our mother's daughters. And no matter how full our mothers' lives have become once their maternal nests have emptied, they will always be our mothers.

—Elizabeth Bookser Barkley, *Woman to Woman: Seeing God in Daily Life*

## Questions for Reflection

*One of the most difficult things we do as young people is break away from our families, and perhaps the most difficult break can be the one between mother and daughter. How did you handle leaving the nest?*

*How did your relationship with your mother change? Was it difficult for her to let you go? Was it equally difficult to leave her?*

## Building New Relationships With Siblings

Just as children need the time and experience to establish independence from parents, the same can be true about sometimes restricting any long-established patterns among siblings…. Maintaining sibling relations takes time and commitment. We can nurture them or allow them to stagnate, just like friendships or marriages. But whether we welcome or resist them, there's no extricating ourselves from the common threads that weave our siblings into the intricate and often complicated web of our adult family lives.

—Elizabeth Bookser Barkley, *Woman to Woman: Seeing God in Daily Life*

## Questions for Reflection

*How have you broken down old walls, conflicts, and resentments and built new positive, uplifting relationships? Are you still trapped in the past? Why?*

*Do you still treat your siblings as the young children or the teenagers you remember them to be? Do they treat you the same way? What steps can you take to meet them where they are today?*

## Building Up Our Own Temple

The human body, precious because God chose to redeem us as the Word incarnate, has rightly been called a temple. But temples should be precious not for themselves, but for the treasures they enshrine. Too many of us confuse the temple with the treasure. Occasionally, we need to distance ourselves from our scales, our exercise bikes, our calorie counters. True, none of these is essentially harmful, but collectively they distract us from a more fulfilling and sacred mission in life: unearthing and sharing the true treasure within us.

—Elizabeth Bookser Barkley, *Woman to Woman: Seeing God in Daily Life*

## Questions for Reflection

*Do you often find yourself tearing your body to pieces? Do you starve yourself or deny yourself healthy food in an attempt to get thinner? Do you spend hours in the gym, trying to attain the perfect body? Why? What would it take to accept your body as it is?*

*How can you build yourself up, and be healthy doing so, without obsessing about your body and self-image?*

## Breaking Down the Dam

The belief that we are somehow, and always, at fault is a very effective way to block God's love for us. Scrupulosity, perfectionism, self-hatred, and depression can all result from this assumption. In John's Gospel, chapter four, Jesus spoke of "living water" flowing from within us. The belief that it's all our fault acts as a huge dam blocking that flow. It will cripple us over and over again, every time we begin to draw closer to God.

—Susan K. Rowland, *Healing After Divorce: Hope for Catholics*

## Questions for Reflection

*What is keeping you from God today? Do you have difficulty reaching out and asking for help? Do you find it difficult to admit you don't have it all "under control" or that everything isn't "perfect"?*

*What is one thing you can do today to break the dam and let the waters "flow" through you again?*

# A Time to Weep, A Time to Laugh

For his anger is but for a moment;
his favor is for a lifetime.
Weeping may linger for the night,
but joy comes with the morning.
(Psalm 30:5)

Blessed are you who weep now, for you will laugh.
Blessed are you when people hate you, and when they exclude you,
revile you, and defame you on account of the Son of Man.
Rejoice in that day and leap for joy, for surely your reward is great
in heaven; for that is what their ancestors did to the prophets.
(Luke 6:21–23)

## Reflection

*People often remark that they are grateful for the sad times in their lives, for without them they would not appreciate the joyous times. But, both of these feelings—joy and pain—and our reactions to them—laughing and weeping—are fleeting. While they are ephemeral, they are also powerful moments in our lives that leave lasting impressions and often change us every time we* experience them. *Whether it is the joyous birth of a child, or the sorrowful letting go of a loved one; whether it is good laughs shared with friends, or the bittersweet good-bye that ends in tears, we should embrace and be grateful for both because, as we know, they only last for a little while.*

. . . . .

*Good Words*

. . . . .

**Uniting Souls With Joy and Sorrow**

We have become deep women, women who have united in our souls the joys and sorrows of life. We are women whose faces wear the grooves of weeping and the lines of laughter. We are women who no longer define our lives by goals won or perfection attained. Women of wisdom are women at peace with the complexities of themselves and the complexities of life.

—Joan Mueller, *Living a Spirituality of Action: A Woman's Perspective*

**Questions for Reflection**

*Think of some of the most joyful moments of your life. Who was a part of these times? Have you given thanks to God for these people or these moments?*

*How has joy colored your perspective of sorrow and vice versa? Are you able to recognize that without sorrow, you would not feel or experience joy in the same way?*

## Comforting the Broken-Hearted

Our instincts don't serve us well with weeping adults. Because we feel helpless, we try to stop the flood with words, and often our words are not chosen well. The God in whose image we are made knows better. Centuries ago, the prophet Isaiah described someone who was to come in God's name with these words:

> The spirit of the LORD GOD is upon me,
>> because the LORD has anointed me;
> he has sent me to bring good news to the oppressed,
>> to bind up the broken-hearted,
>
> . . .
>
> To comfort all who mourn. (Isaiah, 61:1, 2)
> —Carol Luebering, *Coping With Loss: Praying Your Way to Acceptance*

## Questions for Reflection

*Is crying difficult for you to do? Have you been taught that crying is a sign of weakness?*

*Contemplate the words of Isaiah—do you find comfort in your Lord God? Do you feel his embrace as you mourn and weep?*

## Healing the Brokenness Within

Many years ago, I heard an Advent homily.... The priest...dwelt on the first Christ encounter, at Christmastime, taking note of the depression that so many people feel at this time. He said that may be because the outward festive signs do not correspond to our inner feelings. His remedy was for each of us to reconcile the brokenness within so there is something for us to celebrate. That something is wholeness. That something is love, wherever we experience it.

—Dolores R. Leckey, *Grieving With Grace: A Woman's Perspective*

## Questions for Reflection

*It often occurs around the holidays—everyone is happy, joyful, and singing, and you just can't seem to muster the same enthusiasm. And it's not just at the holidays. Perhaps you have been at a friend's baby shower, and you feel nothing but resentment, because you weren't thrown a shower when you were pregnant. Perhaps you've been at weddings and looked on as happy couples twirled and danced, but because of your own heartbreak or loneliness you could not celebrate. Have you ever felt such times of "brokenness"? Do you wish you behaved differently in retrospect? Do you owe others apologies for your behavior?*

## Finding Joy and Laughter in God's Creatures

Francis observed God's creatures, and learned from them. From the birds, he realized that he had the responsibility to preach to them, to care for them, to share his essential identity as creatures of God with them. From the earthworm, he learned humility. He lived simply and close to the soil and the earth. From the bees he learned community, conviviality.

—Ilia Delio, O.S.F., Keith Douglass Warner, O.F.M., and Pamela Wood, *Care for Creation: A Franciscan Spirituality of the Earth*

## Questions for Reflection

*Do you experience joy in nature? Have you ever found yourself laughing at something a pet did or at a squirrel filling his face with nuts? Have you ever smiled at the sight of monkeys swinging from branches, river otters holding hands as they swim, or a mama gorilla holding her baby at the zoo?*

*What are the things in nature that are marvelous, wondrous, miraculous, and joyous? How can you capture more moments of appreciation for God's creation every day?*

## Laugh, Love, and Give Ourselves to a Purpose

Each of us has one distinct life to live. On our life journey we will suffer, laugh, love passionately and give ourselves to a purpose. We will discover our lives are interwoven with one another and that we are called to respond generously to those in need. We offer mercy to the world with our resources and treasures that multiply over time.

—Pegge Bernecker, *Your Spiritual Garden: Tending to the Presence of God*

## Questions for Reflection

*When was the last time you laughed? What was it about?*

*Do you make a point to find joy and laughter in your daily life?*

*What role does laughter play in your purpose in life? Is one of your purposes to bring joy and happiness to others? How do you do it?*

## Taking Yourself Lightly

More familiar to us is [G.K.] Chesterton's remark that angels can fly "because they take themselves lightly." As we smile at this apparently artless aside, we realize that Chesterton was reminding us of another closer-to-home category of beings who wear life more like butterfly wings than a Puritan's wool cloak.

—Gloria Hutchinson, *Be Comforted: Healing in Times of Loss, Anger, Anxiety, Loneliness, Sickness, Death*

## Questions for Reflection

*Are you able to laugh at yourself?*

*Are you always a bit dour and serious? Do others have a difficult time joking with you? What can you do to be more fun to be around?*

## Embracing the Child Within

If whenever we are weighted with worry, we were to find the nearest group of small children and watch them at play, might we remember the words of our Teacher? "Whoever does not receive the kingdom of God as a little child will never enter it" (Mark 10:15).

—Gloria Hutchinson, *Be Comforted: Healing in Times of Loss, Anger, Anxiety, Loneliness, Sickness, Death*

## Questions for Reflection

*Do you watch children play? What do you find shocking about how they interact? Are they guarded? Do they question why they are doing certain things? Do they worry that playing will get in the way of their "to-do" list? Probably not. How can you play more like a child?*

*Why are children so important to our understanding of joy and laughter? What is it about being a child or being around children that makes one feel joyful? What do children have that adults don't? Or vice versa?*

## A Time to Mourn, A Time to Dance

. . . . .

David danced before the LORD with all his might…
(2 Samuel 6:14)

Praise him with tambourine and dance;
praise him with strings and pipe!
(Psalm 150:4)

But to what will I compare this generation? It is like children sitting
in the market-places and calling to one another,
"We played the flute for you, and you did not dance;
we wailed, and you did not mourn."
(Matthew 11:16–17)

### Reflection

*It might surprise you to know some—even Christian—religions ban any
form of dance. And yet, in our own Scriptures, we have a message sent
directly from God telling us to offer praise with music and dance. David
danced before the Lord. In the New Testament Jesus even alludes to the natu-*

ral order of things in a parable when he describes how when children play their flutes they expect others to dance. Jesus himself celebrated with others, and knew there was a time and place for dancing and singing, as there was for mourning and weeping.

Dance, sing, and rejoice! For there will be plenty of time in life for solemnity, silence, and sorrow.

. . . . .
## *Good Words*
. . . . .

### Body and Spirit in Unison

[T]hough everyone can play, not everyone is an athlete. Not everyone has competed in a sport, not everyone's body functions as it once did due to age, injury, circumstance. You may not want to be an athlete…. If you believe in the world of the spiritual and you believe in the world of the flesh and you believe that the two are mysteriously in unison through Christ's redemption, then you don't have to be an athlete to find meaning in these words.

—Susan Saint Sing, *Spirituality of Sport: Balancing Body and Soul*

### Questions for Reflection

*Do you believe the body and spirit are intertwined? How so?*

*If you have let yourself go physically over the years, how is it reflected in your spirituality? Do you find yourself rationalizing your inactivity by saying things like, "I just don't have the time" or, "I am not as young as I used to be"? What keeps you from being in touch with your physical-spiritual being? What is holding you back?*

## Body/Spirit/Mind/Soul Concept

The fluid nature of water is integral to understanding our journey. There is a flow, a soft edge to the meaning of "body, mind, spirit" that will often flow into the holistic "body and soul" metaphor. Allow your understanding to go beyond the individual words, to see body/spirit/mind/soul—as a whole concept, reduced for convenience to body and soul.

—Susan Saint Sing, *Spirituality of Sport: Balancing Body and Soul*

## Questions for Reflection

*Think about the words* body, spirit, mind, *and* soul *a moment. Then think of them together as a "concept"—how does the body depend on the mind, spirit, and soul for sustenance? How does the mind rely on the body for fuel, energy, and health? How do your energy and spirit rely upon your body and mind?*

*Have you sacrificed your mind and spirit at the expense of attaining a perfect body? Or have you focused only on academic and mental pursuits at the expense of your body? Where do your spirit and soul fit in?*

## What It Means to Be Alive!

"Body and soul" is a metaphor acknowledging the spiritual, just as "blood, sweat and tears" is a metaphor for the purely mortal. When we experience the union and force of both these worlds—flesh and spirit—we glimpse the miracle of the Resurrection, we know, for an instant, what Christ felt when he opened his eyes on that slab in the tomb—fully human and fully God—the surge for a second of exuberance, jubilation, joy! To be alive, to breathe and sense every cell of the body responding, *living*.

—Susan Saint Sing, *Spirituality of Sport: Balancing Body and Soul*

## Questions for Reflection

*When was the last time you felt most alive? What were you doing?*

*What can you do today that will marry your body and spirit together and that will make you feel at once active, present, joyful—and alive?*

## Be Beautiful

In the spiritual life, the broader canvas for beauty includes the practice of the virtues. To live as we are meant to live—made in God's image and invited into God's presence—is a beautiful thing to be enjoyed and celebrated. How often do we perceive a life marked by kindness, patience, compassion, humor, righteous anger, peace or courage as something of exquisite beauty? Not only are we beautiful when we are good, but being good engenders a deeper sensitivity to beauty in all its forms.

—Elizabeth A. Dreyer, *Making Sense of God: A Woman's Perspective*

## Questions for Reflection

*Are you living as you are meant to—in God's image and presence?*

*Are you enjoying yourself and celebrating your life? What do you do to honor or celebrate true beauty—"kindness, patience, compassion, humor, righteous anger, peace or courage"?*

## Finding the Element of "Wow!" in Everything

Learning how to take pleasure in the large and small things of life is part of learning how to become a saint. This skill allows our sense of awe and wonder to blossom. Every authentic spiritual life contains an element of "Wow!" And from wonder springs gratitude. To live life as "Thank you" rather than as "You owe me" spares us the inevitable anger and resentment when the world fails to deliver what we demanded. The world does not "owe" us anything. The world is a gift of God.

—Elizabeth A. Dreyer, *Making Sense of God: A Woman's Perspective*

## Questions for Reflection

*What pleasure have you experienced today? Was it in a "small" thing or a "large" thing?*

*Are you living life as a "Thank you" rather than a "You owe me"? How? How can you be better at recognizing life's "Wow!" moments and at being more gracious?*

## Remaining Present in the Moment

Do we miss the "dancing" times because we are worrying about the "mourning" times that may or may not happen? Let's not miss the dance because we are not paying attention to the present.

—Susan K. Rowland, *Make Room for God: Clearing Out the Clutter*

## Questions for Reflection

*Have you ever missed a joyous occasion, because worry or fear got in the way? What are you most afraid of?*

*Do you ever just let go completely and enjoy yourself even though you know that in doing so, pain or hurt is inevitable?*

*What can you do today to feel more present and engaged in life?*

## A Fruit of the Spirit

A fruit of the Spirit is joy. Those who seek God's love through marriage will find joy as well. Delight in the presence of the beloved quickens the commitment to marriage. The vowed promise may sustain one through hard times, but the joy and happiness of being merrily accompanied makes fidelity easy. This yoke is light...

—Sidney Callahan, *Creating New Life, Nurturing Families: A Woman's Perspective*

## Questions for Reflection

*Easier said than done. It is often difficult to sustain joy in marriage—in any long-term relationship or friendship. It is easy to be overcome by the day-to-day activities and trivialities of life. What is keeping you from experiencing joy in your marriage, friendships, or in other relationships?*

*What makes you feel "delight" when thinking of a spouse, dear friend, or loved one? What difficulties have you surmounted together that make it possible to experience joy together?*

# A Time to Throw Away Stones, A Time to Gather Stones Together

Even if you are exiled to the ends of the world,
from there the LORD your God will gather you,
and from there he will bring you back.
(Deuteronomy 30:4)

The reaper is already receiving wages and is
gathering fruit for eternal life, so that sower and
reaper may rejoice together.
(John 4:36)

You are the salt of the earth; but if salt has lost its taste,
how can its saltiness be restored? It is no longer good
for anything, but is thrown out and
trampled under foot.
(Matthew 5:13)

## Reflection

If the Bible was handing out superlatives, one of the candidates for "Most Used Verb" would go to the word gather—it is used over four hundred times in the Bible. There is a theme here, of course. More often than not God wants us to gather to celebrate with each other, mourn for one of God's flock that is lost, or come together as a people to help and serve each other.

God is also adamant about another decree—know when to say when. Just as it is important to gather together, it is equally important to throw out and discard what could be harmful to the entire flock. Of course, only God alone can decide who gets thrown into "eternal fire," and God makes it clear time and time again that this job is not for us mortals to do. Our job is to throw out the parts of ourselves—our faults and failings—that harm ourselves, one another, and the gathered flock as a whole. God will decide in the end who is gathered for all eternity, and who is "thrown out."

. . . . .

*Good Words*

. . . . .

## Knowing When and What to Throw Away

Our belongings should not bog us down and make slaves of us. We should be surrounded with beauty, with things reminding us we are God's children.

Anything else should be removed.

So go ahead and clear out!

—Susan K. Rowland, *Make Room for God: Clearing Out the Clutter*

## Questions for Reflection

*There is an adage that says "What we own owns us." Is that true for you? Are you struggling to maintain a life of appearances—do you own an expensive car, a fancy house, high-end clothing? How much joy do these things give you? Are they worth the sacrifice of your hard work and time, perhaps time spent away from family and friends, to attain them?*

*What one or two things could you give to a charitable organization today? Can you make an active commitment to giving a little bit of what you have to others each week?*

### Throwing Your Life Away—One Bad Choice at a Time

What are the consequences of a lifetime of bad choices? What if we choose addiction, abuse of others, self-indulgence? We become someone God never intended us to be. We become wounded, crippled, twisted in spirit. The deep sinner never lives a great life, makes a "death bed confession" and walks merrily into heaven, happy to have bypassed all the disciplines of a faith-filled life. No, if she makes it at all (and it is very difficult to desire eternal life after a lifetime of bad choices), it is a bedraggled, sorry child who sincerely regrets every moment of her earthly life.

—Susan K. Rowland, *Make Room for God: Clearing Out the Clutter*

### Questions for Reflection

*What are some good parts of yourself that you have thrown out over the years? What can you do to "gather" them back up?*

*What bad habits or decisions are you willing to discard today? How do you think this will improve your life?*

## Examining What You Need to Throw Away

How cluttered is your environment? Is your home jam-packed with furniture, knickknacks, appliances, electronics and gadgets? Is every closet and drawer stuffed with odd papers, old bills, faded receipts, magazines, broken toys, outdated clothes, loose marbles and other mysterious objects that you don't even know how they got there in the first place? Does clutter overflow every surface? Do you lose things regularly? Do you feel lost?

—Susan K. Rowland, *Make Room for God: Clearing Out the Clutter*

## Questions for Reflection

*Sounds familiar. Who doesn't have at least one thing in their home that they can afford to toss out? What is the one thing you can eliminate from your life today?*

*Make a list of your possessions, and prioritize them—as "must-haves," "could live with or without," and "absolute must toss outs." How does this make you feel? Do you feel free? Or bogged down by the weight of your possessions?*

## Being Responsible for What We Throw Away

If everyone in the world consumed as much as Americans do, we would need four additional planets full of resources to supply us. But of course, there are no other planets to support these consumptive habits....The fate of humans and that of the rest of creation are the same. The problem is human sinfulness, human greed. We humans are taking more than our share of the Earth's goods, and throwing away too much "waste." So what happens ecologically when a population —people or other creatures—consumes more resources than the Earth can produce?

—Ilia Delio, O.S.F, Keith Douglass Warner, O.F.M., and Pamela Wood, *Care for Creation: A Franciscan Spirituality of the Earth*

## Questions for Reflection

*How much do you throw away or consume each week? Have you even taken an inventory of the amount of trash you produce? How many gallons of gasoline do you use a week? What can you do today to be more aware of the amount of waste you produce?*

*What steps can you take to control the amount you throw away?*

## Embracing Poverty

Our poverty, however, is a forgotten poverty because the sin of self-centeredness has made us "grabbers" and "graspers." That is why conversion is the movement toward poverty because poverty is the basis of authentic humanity. To be a truly human person is to be poor. The poverty of the human person is not economic poverty but ontological poverty, the poverty of being human. Poverty means that human life, from birth to death, hangs on the threads of God's gracious love. While we may enjoy a wealth of goodness today, we may lose that wealth tomorrow. Life is radically contingent; nothing has to be the way it is. Everything is gift.

—Ilia Delio, O.S.F., *Clare of Assisi: A Heart Full of Love*

## Questions for Reflection

*Are you a "grabber" or "grasper"? Do you ever feel satisfied or content with your life as it is? Do you often find yourself wanting more and "comparing up" by looking at others who seem to have more than you do and coveting what they have? Why?*

*Do you ever find yourself saying, "I deserve this," or, "It's not fair that so-and-so makes a lot of money, and I am only scraping by"? Do you ever stop and think that all of wealth is "contingent" and isn't guaranteed? What can you do to feel more grateful and "blessed" with what you have?*

## Remembering God's House

We can follow Francis' example of remembering that the Earth is not our home alone, but is first and foremost God's house. We can build anew bonds of love, care, concern and companionship with not only our human brothers and sisters, but with the house of creation that sustains us and is kin to us all. We can walk in God's Incarnation daily, remembering that the face of the Divine shines through each and every thing, no matter how small or seemingly insignificant. Through creation, the ineffable is made tangible, and we can sense the radiance of God in the beauty of the natural order.

—Ilia Delio, O.S.F., Keith Douglass Warner, O.F.M., and Pamela Wood, *Care for Creation: A Franciscan Spirituality of the Earth*

## Questions for Reflection

*Do you think of the earth as God's house? When you do, how does it change the way you perceive it? Treat it?*

*Do you see the face of the divine in every thing, "no matter how small or seemingly insignificant"? Where in nature do you feel closest to God?*

# A Time to Embrace, A Time to Refrain From Embracing

I come to my garden, my sister, my bride;
I gather my myrrh with my spice,
I eat my honeycomb with my honey,
I drink my wine with my milk.
Eat, friends, drink,
and be drunk with love.
(Song of Solomon 5:1)

When he had finished speaking, he knelt down with them all and prayed. There was much weeping among them all; they embraced Paul and kissed him, grieving especially because of what he had said, that they would not see him again. Then they brought him to the ship.
(Acts 20:36–38)

## Reflection

*We were all welcomed to the world with an embrace. Our mothers or fathers held us just a moment after we were born. And since our birth we have been embraced or embraced others countless times. It's how we say hello and good-bye to dear friends and loved ones.*

*The airport is always a wonderful place to watch people embrace—the soldier who sees his mother for the first time since deployment opens his arms wide as he walks toward her, or the long-distance lover sees his beloved and runs to her. They embrace. They are home. Prodigal sons and daughters do it. Lovers do it. Brothers do it. Sisters do it. Parents and children do it. Friends do it. They embrace, hold, and envelop. If we are truly made in God's image and do as God does, then in a warm embrace we feel God's touch. We are both God's arms who reach out and the child who is held by the father.*

. . . . .

*Good Words*

. . . . .

## Mary and Elizabeth Embrace

Many artistic depictions of the Visitation focus on the same moment: Mary and Elizabeth standing at the threshold of the house, greeting each other with an embrace. Familial bonds, mutual affection, a shared past, present and future—all are expressed through these two women and their open arms…. It represents an openness to community and a willingness to be present to those in need.

—Ginny Kubitz Moyer, *Mary and Me: Catholic Women Reflect on the Mother of God*

## Questions for Reflection

*Think of a lonely person in your life—perhaps a shut-in, an elderly relative, the neighborhood curmudgeon, or the bitter coworker—could you offer him or her a hug? Or reach out in some way other than an actual "embrace" to show that you are open and have a "willingness to be present to those in need?"*

## Living an Active Faith

As so many women have discovered, the Visitation story is a beautiful example of what it means to live an active faith. It reminds us that we're all called to reach out to others, to be present in their struggles and joys. Sometimes this means traveling a physical distance; other times it requires navigating the rocky terrain of our own emotions. Either way, the Visitation proves that even the most difficult journey is worth it, for in each other's embrace we're more than the sum of our parts; we are a community, the very core of the Christian faith. Best of all, when we come together we're giving life to Mary's own son, who is born again in our encounters.

—Ginny Kubitz Moyer, *Mary and Me: Catholic Women Reflect on the Mother of God*

## Questions for Reflection

*In what ways do you live an "active faith"?*

*What can you do today to show that you are willing to reach out to others?*

**Knowing When to Say When, and Knowing God Will Be There**

God knows all the ins and outs of relationships. God knows all the issues we have hidden deep down (even from ourselves) which made us choose the mate we chose. God has seen all our efforts to make it work. God has seen all the denial. God knows our hearts thoroughly. And God loves us, plain and simple, no "buts."

And God often sets us free from marriages that are false, sick, and unworkable.

The spiritual work of a healthily married couple is to discover in their self-giving that same love that God always pours out.

—Susan K. Rowland, *Healing After Divorce: Hope for Catholics*

**Questions for Reflection**

*Ideally, we all hope to kiss and make up. We hope an embrace will solve everything. But, really, we know it can't. Have you ever realized that no matter how much work, love, and dedication you put into a particular relationship, it will end?*

*If you're married, what aspects of your relationships need work? Communication? Intimacy? Respect? Trust? What can you and your spouse do together to embrace your marriage and seek the help you need to sustain it?*

## Embracing Your Marriage

Marriage is the training program into which the vast majority of human beings throughout history have entered to learn about God's love and purpose. This training program tests our patience, our kindness, and selflessness—or our ability to give without counting the cost. As each partner in a healthy marriage grows in love of the other spouse, their love grows for God, whether they are aware of it or not.

—Susan K. Rowland, *Healing After Divorce: Hope for Catholics*

## Questions for Reflection

*What parts of yourself have you embraced in your marriage? What parts of yourself have you let go while married? Do you miss these parts of yourself, or have you changed in a positive, healthy way?*

*Would you consider yours a healthy marriage? Why or why not? What parts of your marriage need work?*

## Embracing Your Full Humanity

Whatever it takes for women to embrace their full humanity—which for Christians is living out the truth that we are made in God's image and likeness—requires courage and involves risk. Courage can be public and social, or quiet and behind the scenes. One size does not fit all. Each of us must decide for herself.

— Elizabeth A. Dreyer, *Making Sense of God: A Woman's Perspective*

## Questions for Reflection

*Have you embraced your full humanity—living the truth that you are made in God's image?*

*What are you meant to do with your life? Are you doing it?*

*Do you have the necessary "courage" to take the risk of doing what you need to do to live more fully human? What is holding you back?*

## Embracing Mature Adulthood

A woman growing into mature adulthood desires to be affirmed in her world—whatever that world is—to speak more with her own voice; to be recognized in her own right not merely as an appendage to her husband, children, parents, or boss. She wants to be, and to be viewed as, independent, competent, and responsible, and to be taken seriously in ways that distinguish adults from children.

—Patricia Cooney Hathaway, *Weaving Faith and Experience:*
*A Woman's Perspective*

## Questions for Reflection

*Do you feel like you are affirmed in your world? Do you have a clear voice—one that people listen to?*

*Do you feel as though you are merely an "appendage" to your husband, children, parents, or boss? Why? What are you doing to make yourself feel like this? How can you "separate" or "refrain from embracing" this identity?*

## Embracing Your World

You can experience compassion, hold someone in the prayer space of your heart, and send loving energy to the four corners of the world in very little time and with very few words. Yet, you are conscious of worldly concerns and of your connectedness with all members of the human family. We've heard the expression, "Think globally; act locally." This phrase applies to a way of being grounded and reaching out, of being limited to one place and embracing any spot on the globe. Developing this perspective has transforming power and contributes to inner peace.

—Clare Wagner, *Awakening to Prayer: A Woman's Perspective*

## Questions for Reflection

*Have you practiced sending "loving energy" to other parts of the world—or other people? Try to do so today. Sit and contemplate others around the world—or perhaps a stranger you often sit next to on the bus or a cashier you often see at the grocery store. Practice sending loving thoughts to them throughout the day. How does it transform you? How do you feel differently toward these people?*

. . . . .
# A Time to Seek, A Time to Lose
. . . . .

From there you will seek the LORD your God, and you will find him
if you search after him with all your heart and soul.
(Deuteronomy 4:29)

For the Son of Man came to seek out and to save the lost.
(Luke 19:10)

## Reflection

*A recurring theme in both the Old and New Testaments is that of searching
and finding, and then losing all over again. How many of us spend our life
searching for God, for meaning, for love, for excitement, for anything? We
seem to be programmed to seek. Even our favorite game as children is Hide
and Seek. Yes, we're all searching for something. Often, though, we're looking for love in all the wrong places. And we sometimes spend an inordinate
amount of time searching for God and wondering if God's out there at all. If
we stopped for a moment, we might discover God has been with us the entire
time. But, sometimes it takes loss to appreciate and understand the supreme
joy of finding something again. And God knows that better than anyone.
Time and time again, we have run off and gotten lost, and when he finds us
again, like the father hugged his Prodigal Son, he embraces us and rejoices:
You were lost and now are found!*

*Good Words*

**Finding Your True Calling**

Whatever your age, today finds you with a treasure chest of hopes and dreams. Hopefully you have realized many of the dreams you held as a child. But perhaps you still experience a longing for unrealized treasures that resides in your heart. One way you can realize your dreams is if you identify your vocation in life and begin to share that vocation with others—through your time, talent, values and good works. Knowing your identity and calling allows you to give others your material and spiritual treasures and, in the meantime, realize your dreams.

—Pegge Bernecker, *Your Spiritual Garden: Tending to the Presence of God*

**Questions for Reflection**

*What do you want to be when you grow up? You often heard this question as a child, but no one asks this question of adults. Is it ever too late to start over? To do what you were truly meant to do?*

## When Loss Hurts

Loss hurts. It hurts all the time. It monopolizes your attention. The pain takes many forms. It may be sharp as a knife, cutting your soul in two. It may be a dull ache that never quite goes away. It rolls over you in unexpected waves. You may find yourself bursting into tears without warning—or you may wish you could cry and wash the hurt out.

…When we lose someone we love, we lose a piece of ourselves, and the loss leaves a gaping, throbbing wound.

—Carol Luebering, *Coping With Loss: Praying Your Way to Acceptance*

## Questions for Reflection

*The most painful loss to endure is that of a loved one. It seems incomprehensible that we should have to lose people we love. Yet, we all do. Why do you think "loss" of this kind is necessary to the human experience?*

*What did the loss of a loved one teach you about living your life?*

## Seeking and Finding Your True Self

The humble woman lets her light shine! She will look at the opportunity for a promotion and say, "I've been the top sales representative for over a year. I know our clientele inside and out, and I think others can learn a lot from my experience. I'm committed to providing great customer service, and perhaps the best way to utilize my skills is by managing newer members of the sales team." Likewise she can also say, "I'm a good piano player, but I'm not meant to be a concert pianist. There is something very freeing about acknowledging that. It takes off the pressure to spend hours in rehearsal, and music becomes a joy when I'm asked to play for friends."

—Beth M. Knobbe, *Finding My Voice: A Young Woman's Perspective*

## Questions for Reflection

*How can you let your light shine today?*

*What self-identifier can you afford to lose? Like the pianist above who acknowledges she will never be a concern pianist and can now just relax and enjoy playing, what identity are you holding on to? What's keeping you from just relaxing and enjoying your life?*

## Finding Our True Selves

There is no right or wrong way to go about discovering who we are. We discover who we are by trying new things, paying attention to what feels right, naming things that we're good at, and listening for what other people affirm in us. It happens through prayer, reflection, and by listening for the call from within. Finding our true self certainly does not happen without daring to dream and taking some risks. We are free to choose our own career, our friends, our interests. God leaves us free to be whatever we like. By becoming who we are in our fullness, we give glory to God.

—Beth M. Knobbe, *Finding My Voice: A Young Woman's Perspective*

## Questions for Reflection

*Recall a moment when you felt you were doing exactly what you were called to do. How did you feel? What were you doing? How can you feel that way again?*

*Can you name the things you are good at? What stands out?*

## Seeking Acceptance

The goal, the long-sought gift of peace, is acceptance. It does not arise suddenly, like the sun bursting through the rain clouds. Rather, we reach it slowly and gradually. We begin to realize that the unthinkable loss has truly occurred. Sorrow becomes a less constant ache and the clouds of depression lift....

Acceptance is one of the gifts with which God loves to shower us.

—Carol Luebering, *Coping With Loss: Praying Your Way to Acceptance*

## Questions for Reflection

*In what areas of your life are you seeking acceptance? Do you need to accept the loss of a friend, loved one, child?*

*What part of your life do you have the most difficulty accepting? What can you do to take a step toward acceptance and peace?*

## Being True to the Self

It is vital that women have a solid sense of self to bring *to* relationships rather than a fragile sense of self that continually changes depending upon what others want us to be or do for them. To find a balance between caring for self while also attending to the needs of others are two facets of the challenge women face in becoming their own persons.

—Patricia Cooney Hathaway, *Weaving Faith and Experience: A Woman's Perspective*

## Questions for Reflection

*Part of finding yourself usually entails trying new things. However, have you ever found yourself doing something you didn't enjoy for the sake of another, so much so that you lost yourself in the process?*

*In relationships, how much of yourself do you lose to make the other person happy? Yes, there is compromise in any relationship, but do you feel as though others do not reciprocate?*

*What can you do or say to articulate to others what it is that you want to do?*

. . . . .

# A Time to Keep, A Time to Throw Away

. . . . .

On that day people will throw away
to the moles and to the bats
their idols of silver and their idols of gold,
which they made for themselves to worship.
(Isaiah 2:20)

Rejoice always, pray without ceasing, give thanks in all
circumstances; for this is the will of God in Christ
Jesus for you. Do not quench the Spirit. Do not
despise the words of prophets, but test everything;
hold fast to what is good; abstain from every form of evil.
(1 Thessalonians 5:16–22)

## Reflection

*There are plenty of things in life we should keep. "Hold fast" to everything that is good, beautiful, life-fulfilling, the Scripture says. But abstain or throw out evil, or the things that keep us from living the life God intended for us. Isaiah warns that on judgment day we will throw away the idols we have made out of our earthly possessions—but why wait? What in your life should you be holding on to, and what should you be throwing out today?*

. . . . .
*Good Words*
. . . . .

## Hold On to What Is Beautiful and Good

Beauty not only sustains us. It has the capability of saving us from despair and from wanting to close our eyes in the face of difficulty. A reason to be awake is to not miss the beauty. Without denying ugliness and even the destructive aspect of nature, the beauty of creation and of gifts which flow from the creative minds and hearts of human beings are astounding in their power to sustain and uplift.

—Clare Wagner, *Awakening to Prayer: A Woman's Perspective*

## Questions for Reflection

*Go outside today and admire God's creation. What strikes you as beautiful?*

*How can you capture the beauty you see around you and keep it with you without physically touching it?*

## Embracing the Theology of Creation

With awareness of earth's wounds and fragility because of our misuse, we awaken anew to her beauty. Awareness of the earth as magnificent gift is flowering among scientists, poets, spiritual seekers, and even political leaders across the world. Jesus used the mustard seed, the lilies of the field, living water, the sower and the seed, the birds of the air, and other creation images to communicate his understanding of God and sacredness in life. The medieval mystics grounded their mystical sensibilities in a theology of creation.

—Clare Wagner, *Awakening to Prayer: A Woman's Perspective*

## Questions for Reflection

*How have you misused creation? What have you done to throw out what is good and damage what is beautiful? How can you make amends?*

*How do you contribute to keeping the world beautiful?*

## Holding Fast to What Is Good

[Clare of Assisi] described the crucified Christ as a mirror because in gazing upon this mirror we see a true reflection of ourselves—our image. Christ reflects back to us what we are to be in our lives. The notion of the mirror to describe who we are in reaction to God is a profound one because mirrors are such an integral part of our everyday lives. The mirror reveals to us how we look.

—Ilia Delio, O.S.F., *Clare of Assisi: A Heart Full of Love*

## Questions for Reflection

*What do you see when you look in the mirror? Do you see yourself as part of God's beautiful creation?*

*What parts of yourself (both inside and out) do you wish you could keep? Why do you find these parts beautiful? For example, do you have your mother's color or shape of eyes? When you look in them do you see her? Do you share the same crooked smile as your child? Does it make you happy to see that parts of you are connected to parts of others whom you love? Does it help you accept who you are?*

## Gazing at Our True Selves

...[The] mirrors we peer into in our everyday world give us a glimpse of ourselves, we see only the exterior image and not the full image of who we are; the image we see is incomplete. What if we had mirrors that allowed us to look within ourselves as well? What if we peered into a mirror that reflected our hearts, minds or souls? What would we see and would we like what we see? Clare asks Agnes of Prague to gaze into the mirror of the crucified Christ so as to discover who she is inwardly and what she reflects outwardly. Only in the mirror of the cross, Clare indicates, do we truly see who we are and what we are called to be by becoming transformed into the image of Christ.

—Ilia Delio, O.S.F., *Clare of Assisi: A Heart Full of Love*

## Questions for Reflection

*Clare says to gaze upon, consider, contemplate, and imitate the Crucified Christ in order to be transformed. In doing so, you will change your heart, mind, and soul. Instead of gazing in the mirror to recognize your physical beauty or perceived ugliness, have you tried gazing upon Christ? What happens?*

*What parts of yourself do you see when you consider and contemplate Christ? What parts do you want to keep? What parts are you willing to throw away?*

## Identifying Your Gifts

One way to identify how we might make a difference is to take a realistic inventory of our gifts. Gifts are not necessarily skills that come with official papers. Some of us have diplomas and certifications —these are treasured, acquired skills—but we may also have gifts that we rarely consider....

Sometimes it is the skills that seem least valuable that make the most difference in effecting change in the world.... It is important to recognize one's gifts. Working through an inventory of gifts may be helpful as it encourages us to discover not only professional skills, but also those that bring healing and comfort to others.

—Joan Mueller, *Living a Spirituality of Action: A Woman's Perspective*

## Questions for Reflection

*Create an inventory of your gifts, accomplishments, and attributes. Decide which ones you will keep, and continue to work on. Are you surprised by how many gifts you have been blessed with in life?*

*Create inventories for your friends and loved ones as well. Let people know how much you value and respect all that they bring to your life and the lives others. Tell them to keep it up.*

## Embracing Spiritual Poverty

Economic poverty is not difficult to attain. Spiritual poverty, however, can be. It means relinquishing that which we possess to smother the ego or barricade it against the intrusion of others. It is the antidote to human violence, to the need to assert ourselves over and over and against others. Gazing upon the poor crucified Christ gave Clare [of Assisi] insight into the human person. She realized that becoming poor is not contrary to the fulfillment of human nature but rather the very fulfillment of our humanity. Christ reveals to us that the human person is poor by nature.

—Ilia Delio, O.S.F., *Clare of Assisi: A Heart Full of Love*

## Questions for Reflection

*It is quite possibly one of the most difficult aspects of Christianity—to embrace poverty. Are you willing to live with little, so that others who have nothing may have a little too?*

*Why do you feel so attached to your earthly possessions? Do you feel bogged down by your need to possess more? What in your spirit is lacking that creates this hunger for more stuff?*

## Throwing Out the Stuff That Gets in the Way

There is a comfort in the stuff we collect. It can feel like a fluffy old quilt to wrap ourselves in when the world gets to be too much.

But the things we keep have a downside: They turn on us. Things start falling out of closets on our heads. We can't find the key or the wallet or the checkbook. We become allergic to the dust, and we can't keep the house clean. New items don't fit into any drawer or closet.

Clutter steals away our time and saps our energy. It takes time and energy to keep it, to take care of it, to find things we need buried under it.

—Susan K. Rowland, *Make Room for God: Clearing out the Clutter*

## Questions for Reflection

*Have your possessions turned on you? Have you begun to lose things? Are you unable to keep track of all you own and all of your expenses?*

*How has the stuff you own taken over your life? Do you spend an inordinate amount of time acquiring new stuff, only to find yourself spending more time taking care of it, or worse, forgetting about it altogether and moving on to the next thing?*

· · · · ·
## *A Time to Tear, A Time to Sew*
· · · · ·

And on the seventh day God finished the work that he had done,
and he rested on the seventh day from all the work he had done.
(Genesis 2:2)

Simon answered, "Master, we have worked all night long but have
caught nothing. Yet if you say so, I will let down the nets."
(Luke 5:5)

But Martha was distracted by her many tasks; so she came to him
and asked, "Lord, do you not care that my sister has left me to do
all the work by myself? Tell her then to help me."
(Luke 10:40)

### Reflection
*Work. Work. Work. We all do it. Every day there is a long list of tasks
we must accomplish just to survive—and to help our loved ones survive.
There can be nothing more frustrating than working all day, sometimes all
night too, perhaps even for years and years, and having seemingly little to
show for it. How many times have you spent hours working, only to have*

it dismissed or torn apart by a coworker, child, or spouse? How many hours did you work, only to discover there simply isn't enough time in the day to do all you still have to do? How often have you worked, and like Martha and the Prodigal Son's brother, watched as others received the rewards for it? We are all seamstresses of sorts. Our work is to create something even though we know eventually it will be torn. Yes, our work will be undone. But as Jesus says, "My Father is still working, and I also am working" (John 5:17). So must we.

. . . . .
## *Good Words*
. . . . .

### Working Smarter, Not Harder

Bees get a lot of work done. They fly great distances to find the kind of nectar they need to bring back to the hive. The honey they make is valuable not only to them but to others who appreciate its food value and sweetness. Bees rarely bang their heads against rocks. If there is something in their path, they simply fly around it. They don't make the rock a cause. They don't go to war against it. They don't waste energy on it at all.

Sometimes our efforts fit and sometimes they don't. Making ourselves fit, forcing a fit, is not helpful....

—Joan Mueller, *Living a Spirituality of Action: A Woman's Perspective*

### Questions for Reflection

*Do you find yourself fighting "rocks" during the day, instead of going around them?*

*Do you show others your appreciation for the work they do? Or are you a "rock," sapping others of their time and energy by being overly judgmental? How can you help others with their work instead of getting in their way?*

## Being Open to Change in the Workplace

In "getting out there" we can take a lesson from the bees. We may have to fly around rocks, go from one flower to another with ease until we find a place where what we have to offer is needed. This requires a certain freedom to try a number of things before landing....

Everything we try won't work, but if we try enough things and strategically think about what we propose, we will make a difference.

—Joan Mueller, *Living a Spirituality of Action: A Woman's Perspective*

## Questions for Reflection

*In Luke 5:5, Simon basically says to Jesus, "Hey, I've been working here all day—like I always have. Now what? What makes you think throwing my nets in this way, will produce more fish? But if you say so...". We've all been there. Have you ever heard yourself saying, "Well, that's the way I've always done it"? When a coworker shows you how to do something new or different, is your first reaction to dismiss it? Or like Simon, despite your doubts, do you cast your net?*

## Finding God in the Workplace

For many of us the most difficult place to find God is in our work. Can it truly be an avenue of God's grace? While our spirituality can be personal, it cannot be private. As disciples of Jesus, all of us are called to bring gospel values of peace, justice, and love not only into our homes, but also into the workplace....

—Patricia Cooney Hathaway, *Weaving Faith and Experience:*
*A Woman's Perspective*

## Questions for Reflection

*How do you live the gospel values at work? Do you refrain from gossip or judgment? Are you supportive and compassionate? Are you humble, and seek the least possible praise or accolades from others, but mete it out generously to coworkers and peers?*

*Do speak kindly to everyone? Do you make a point to compliment people and make them feel good about themselves and the job they are doing? Do you make yourself open and available to all of your coworkers and never snub anyone because they do not share the same rank as you?*

## Work as Ministry

Many women have spoken to me about the sense of meaning they receive when they view their work as ministry. They describe going about their normal activities with the intention of serving God through the people and tasks of their day....

Yet, others have described their work as drudgery, as a source of stress and a drain on their energy, something they resent and do not look forward to. Yet, if that work, as difficult as it is, is undertaken for the honor and glory of God—God will bless it and bring some good out of it.

—Patricia Cooney Hathaway, *Weaving Faith and Experience:*
*A Woman's Perspective*

## Questions for Reflection

*In what ways is your work ministry? Do you serve people, customers, other employees? Do you treat all people with respect, love, and dignity? Do you lead by example, and live out the gospel in all your interactions?*

*What is one thing you can do every day at the workplace to live out the gospel?*

## Realizing Your True Self at Work

Women also desire to be affirmed not only for qualities long associated with the feminine—generosity, empathy, and compassion—but also for qualities associated with masculinity—ambition, leadership skills, and intellectual competence. An important goal for women in their forties and fifties is the integration of both sets of qualities within each person in the realization of the true self.

—Patricia Cooney Hathaway, *Weaving Faith and Experience: A Woman's Perspective*

## Questions for Reflection

*How important to you is it that you are associated with the qualities of ambition, leadership, and intelligence?*

*Do you think ambition has a place in living the gospel life? In what capacity?*

. . . . .

## *A Time to Keep Silence, A Time to Speak*

. . . . .

Those who speak on their own seek their own glory;
but the one who seeks the glory of him who sent him is true,
and there is nothing false in him.

(John 7:18)

For it is God's will that by doing right you should silence the
ignorance of the foolish. As servants of God, live as free people,
yet do not use your freedom as a pretext for evil. Honor everyone.
Love the family of believers. Fear God. Honor the emperor.

(1 Peter 2:15–17)

**Reflection**

*Knowing when to speak and when not to is probably one of the most precious skills a person can possess. And by the looks of the state of the world, it's a gift few have practiced and mastered! We all seem to think what we have to say is of utmost importance—"No one could possibly be as brilliant as me!" We think others are hanging on our every word. Sometimes we think we have other people figured out and take it upon ourselves to talk about them, psychoanalyzing them, predicting their behavior, or reminiscing about their mistakes—in other words, gossiping about them. Sometimes we think we need to be "honest" with a friend and tell her "just what she needs to hear." When, in fact, the only advice we're qualified to mete out is—none. But, there are times and places when we should share our thoughts and use our voices. Yes, there is a time to speak, especially for those who can't speak for themselves. But, more often than not, we can spread the gospel without speaking, and as Saint Francis advised, only when necessary "use words." In other words, action speaks louder. Shh!*

. . . . .
*Good Words*
. . . . .

## Speaking Up for Those Who Can't

The virtue of courage is a gift. It is the ability to affirm life in the face of death or non-being. When women experience marginalization in family, society, or church, or when they witness the imposition of invisibility on others, it is time to take a deep breath and muster the courage to stand up, speak out, and challenge the status quo. Speaking up is doubly difficult for persons who have been consistently rendered voiceless.

—Elizabeth A. Dreyer, *Making Sense of God: A Woman's Perspective*

## Questions for Reflection

*In what ways do you give a voice to the voiceless? An unborn child? The poor? The abused? The downtrodden?*

*Is there a problem in society you feel especially passionate about, but are afraid to speak out on because you are worried about what others will think of you? Why?*

## Embracing the Silence

Having an empty nest makes it much easier for me to live in more silence. I don't have my son coming and going with his music and his friends in tow asking what there is to eat. I certainly enjoyed those days, but they are gone. I rarely turn on the television during the day, and I live in the country with enough seclusion that the noises of the world are muted. I am fortunate, and I have come to prefer the quiet in a deep sort of way, like preferring a thick, homemade vegetable soup to a fast-food hamburger. Silence is delicious, sustaining and health-giving.

—Lyn Holley Doucet, *Healing Troubled Hearts: Daily Spiritual Exercises*

## Questions for Reflection

*Try to sit alone in a quiet place. How does it make you feel? Do you feel rested and transformed?*

*Do you miss silence? Are you surrounded by other people's chatter all day? Do you come home to a bustling household filled with people, music, and talking? What can you do to find a silent retreat? Where would you like to go?*

## Listening to the Cries of Your Soul

I even feel a little disconcerted now when I go into a noisy house with one or two televisions going, Game Boys popping and telephones ringing constantly. I confess to wanting to control another's space! I want to reach out and turn things off! However, I understand that this is the reality that many, maybe most, families in our country live with. We have grown accustomed to higher levels of noise, and lots and lots of activity. This impacts us all....

Yet the truth is that all this noise and activity drowns out God's silent and still voice, the voice that drifts in on the gentlest of breezes. We no longer hear the cries of our own souls.

—Lyn Holley Doucet, *Healing Troubled Hearts: Daily Spiritual Exercises*

## Questions for Reflection

*Where do you feel most disconcerted? Are you in a room with a lot of electronics? A restaurant filled with people? A store packed with people and music playing in the background? What can you do to cope with the situation if you have little control over it? Take a mental snapshot of your surroundings the next time you feel stressed and tense. Do this over several days. At the end of the week, try to determine if the common denominator to your stress and frustration had to do with the lack of silence and peace.*

## The Truth Will Set You Free

Jesus didn't have to be God to know what would happen to him if he kept preaching. He knew how the world treated those who stood fast in a truth not ready to be heard. But he spoke out anyway because he knew his truth would set us free. The Son of God came in truth and love to set us free so that we could reclaim our place as children of God.

—Judith Dunlap, *Bringing Home the Gospel: The Year of Matthew*

## Questions for Reflection

*Have you ever been persecuted for your beliefs? If not, would you be willing, like Christ, to risk your life for them?*

*Think of all the courageous people and saints in history who spoke out in defense of their faith, their belief in humanity, and their dedication to the truth. Who do you most admire? Why? What qualities in this person do you wish you could possess?*

## The Resurrection Within

When our foremothers went to jail to secure the right to vote not only for themselves but for future generations, that was resurrection. When a battered wife finds the courage to leave an abusive situation, that's resurrection. When a woman in midlife decides to follow her dream of studying the violin, that's resurrection. When Elizabeth Ann Seton, Catherine McAuley, and a host of founders of communities of women religious followed their inner voice that urged something new—that was resurrection. We need to sharpen our attentiveness to the signs of resurrection all around us, and within us.

—Dolores R. Leckey, *Grieving With Grace: A Woman's Perspective*

## Questions for Reflection

*What resurrection is waiting for you? What is your inner voice urging you to do? Change careers? Leave an abusive relationship? Travel? Learn a new language? Discover a new hobby?*

*What are some visible signs of resurrection that are all around you? If you have had a similar resurrection in your life already what were those signs? What made you pay attention to them?*

. . . . .

# A Time to Love, A Time to Hate

. . . . .

You have heard that it was said, "You shall love your neighbor and
hate your enemy." But I say to you, Love your enemies and pray
for those who persecute you, so that you may be children of your
Father in heaven; for he makes his sun rise on the evil and on the
good, and sends rain on the righteous and on the unrighteous.

(Matthew 5:43–45)

For this reason the Father loves me, because I lay down my life in
order to take it up again.

(John 10:17)

## Reflection

*"All you need is love," John Lennon sang. But, before Lennon and the
Beatles performed it, Jesus spoke it and lived it. Then he died just to prove it.
Jesus brought the world the most powerful message of all time: The great-
est gift we'll ever receive is love. Love is what our purpose here on earth
is. We are to love one another; our neighbor as ourselves. We are, shocking as this sounds, even supposed to love our enemies, those who hate us,
persecute us, revile us, and utter all types of falsehoods against us. Paul*

later tells us in 1 Corinthians 13, that we are to love unconditionally, patiently, kindly, without jealousy, anger, or resentment. We are to be selfless in all our actions and even, when necessary, lay down our lives for our friends. We are, however, called to hate too. Paul tells us in his letter to the Romans 12:9, "Let love be genuine; hate what is evil, hold fast to what is good...". No, we are not to hate others, we are only supposed to hate and revile evil that could harm others. Hatred and evil are the poison, and love is the antidote.

. . . . .
*Good Words*
. . . . .

## Are You Ready for a Thing Called Love?

Love is praised in all times and all places. Nothing else inspires such heartfelt awe, joy, and passionate deeds. No wonder that poetry, drama, novels, music, philosophy, religion, and science perennially try to understand the mysterious nature of love. What is this thing called love? Does love really make the world go round or move the heavens and the stars? Women who fall in love, marry for love, and love their children do well to ponder the depth of the drama of love they enact upon life's stage.

—Sidney Callahan, *Creating New Life, Nurturing Families:*
*A Woman's Perspective*

## Questions for Reflection

*How do you show or express love? Do you do things for others? Say that you love others? Do you give gifts? Do you write letters or poems? Or some combination of the above?*

*How do you like to receive love? Do you appreciate the words "I love you"? Or do simple gestures matter more to you? How do you like people to express their love to you? How can you communicate how you want to receive love to those you care most about?*

## Truth in Love

In my view it is better to see love in all of its incarnations. Certainly theologians now emphasize that love of God cannot be separated from love of neighbor; Scripture proclaims clearly that to love the invisible God you must love the neighbor that you can see. If not, you are a liar. Conflict between love of God and neighbor does not really make sense but is the ground of all being, all becoming, and all loving. The God of love makes loving possible.

So what is the essence of love? I know it's truly love when I can say yes, yes, and yes again to who or what I love, and embrace the loved person or activity with a heightened aliveness and commitment.

—Sidney Callahan, *Creating New Life, Nurturing Families:*
*A Woman's Perspective*

## Questions for Reflection

*Do you truly love God? And by that, do you truly love all your neighbors—friend and foe?*

*Who is the most difficult person you know? Have you ever heard yourself say that you "hate" this person? Perhaps they have harmed you or a family member? Is it possible for you to forgive him or her? Can you "love" them simply by not hating them or judging them?*

## Love and Sex

Christians today understand that married people should strive to be holy *through, with*, and *in* their sexual life together. A mutually loving embodied self-giving in marriage ideally encompasses both erotic passion and charity. The vowed commitment of marital union is fittingly consummated by sexual intercourse as the couple become "one flesh." Best of all, theologians now assert that each act of intercourse, whether potentially procreative or not, concretely reenacts the loving vowed gift of mutual commitment.

—Sidney Callahan, *Creating New Life, Nurturing Families:*
*A Woman's Perspective*

## Questions for Reflection

*One way married people share and express love is through sex. Do you treat sex as another form of expression of love? Or has it become rote, and more of an obligation?*

*Is sex something you enjoy with your spouse? Have you grown together or apart over the years? Have you made a special point to keep sex part of your marriage? What can you do to improve your sex life?*

## Let's Talk About Sex

The marital bond is strengthened by repeated experiences of love, pleasure, and joy. Love grows strong through practiced expressions embodying sexuality, because one's body has its own nonverbal language of gift. Sexual acts can be recognized as an embodied form of communication that is as potent as the spoken word. Like a language there is a grammar of appropriate expression and an ethic of use: We must say what we mean and mean what we say both sexually and linguistically. Fidelity to love and to the partner is essential as is true speech.

—Sidney Callahan, *Creating New Life, Nurturing Families:*
*A Woman's Perspective*

## Questions for Reflection

*Do you clearly articulate to your spouse what your desires are? Does your spouse express his wishes? How do you both feel about your current sex life?*

*Do you still feel close and "in love"? Are you able to express yourself completely during sex? What is holding you back?*

## Love Is a Mystery

Observance of couples walking around on this earth teaches a valuable truism: Relationships seem very mysterious. How did he get with her? How did she end up with him? How do they make it work? Or don't they? Perhaps most mysterious of all are long-term relationships of forty or more years. Sometimes the two look like they do not even like each other, let alone possess a love strong enough to endure time's travails.

—Donna Erickson Couch, *Together But Alone: When God Means Something Different to Your Spouse*

## Questions for Reflection

*Is love that mysterious? Have you ever found yourself marveling at how love works? Two seemingly mismatched people come together—for life. It's astounding really. What couples do you know that have utterly surprised you by their love for each other? What do you most admire in them?*

*What do you believe makes a solid, lasting, loving relationship? Respect? Trust? Patience? Fidelity? Passion?*

## Passion and Compassion

Mother [Teresa] taught me without love there is no passion or compassion. Without love, life has no meaning. Mother wanted everyone to know God's love and to love God as she did. She told us we are all called to love one another as our Father loves us and she showed us how.

—Maryanne Raphael, *What Mother Teresa Taught Me*

## Questions for Reflection

*What do you think Mother Teresa means by "without love there is no passion or compassion"? Whenever you felt passionately about someone or something, did you stop to think that "love" was the reason behind it all? When you expressed compassion for another person, did you recognize you were "loving" him or her?*

*Does your life have "love" or "meaning" in it? Are you seeking meaning, but really looking for love? Or vice versa? Did you realize you were searching for the same thing?*

*Think of Mother Teresa and her amazing life. How did her life teach you about love? What do you find most inspiring about her life? Could you love as selflessly as she did?*

## One True Love Story

I challenge you to reflect a bit more about the "no marriage in heaven" comment. What statement was Jesus making about the ultimate love relationship, the eternal marriage? We cannot imagine everlasting union. We cannot visualize living anywhere but on this beautiful blue orb called Earth, walking with the ones we love. But if there really is only one love story, then the journey into God, alone and together, is well worth the effort and sacrifices demanded of such a wonderful and mysterious adventure.

—Donna Erickson Couch, *Together But Alone: When God Means Something Different to Your Spouse*

## Questions for Reflection

*How do you feel about there being "no marriage in heaven"?*

*In what ways do you show love to each other, and help each other grow closer to loving God?*

. . . . .

# A Time for War, A Time for Peace

. . . . .

But if you have bitter envy and selfish ambition in your hearts, do
not be boastful and false to the truth....

Those conflicts and disputes among you, where do they come
from? Do they not come from your cravings that are at war within
you? You want something and do not have it; so you commit mur-
der. And you covet something and cannot obtain it; so you engage
in disputes and conflicts.

(James 3:14–4:2)

## Reflection

*It is difficult to rationalize war under the new covenant. Jesus made it clear*
*that with his gospel message the old world order, the one that sanctioned*
*revenge and even war, was over. The only thing people are called to do is*
*to love, Jesus preached. And once everyone learns to coexist and love, even*
*their enemies, then, and only then, will there be peace on earth. Jesus came*
*as one of us to show us the way. He lived his short life loving, healing, and*
*showing compassion, and ultimately he died for us. He warned us time and*
*time again about the sins that lead to conflict and war—jealousy, anger,*

greed, and lack of forgiveness. Most importantly, Jesus lived his message. He never fought back. He did not repay evil for evil. He accepted the nails as they were hammered into his flesh. He felt the blood drip down his head, and did not raise a hand to his oppressors. From the cross, he looked upon all who yelled at him, and asked his Father to forgive them. Jesus lived peace. He died peace. He fought the ultimate war against war, and he did so hanging on a cross and rising three days later—the victorious Paschal Lamb.

·····
*Good Words*
·····

## Choosing Peace

To understand how to live a life of active nonviolence, an understanding of the vocabulary of peacemaking is necessary. A vital differentiation must be made between pacifism (or active nonviolence) and passivity. At the root of true pacifism is the desire to discover peaceful formulas for addressing conflict at all levels.

—Patricia Patten Normile, S.F.O., *John Dear on Peace: An Introduction to His Life and Works*

## Questions for Reflection

*What does it mean to you to practice "active nonviolence"?*

*Do you believe there are times for war? When? What do you believe is the root cause of current wars around the globe?*

### Practicing Active Nonviolence

Yet pacifism in people's minds often connotes passivity. Passivity, when related to peace-seeking, indicates lethargy, an inert state, a tendency to allow the world and its tumultuous events to wash over one without a consideration for what might be done to make the world a more peaceful place. Passivity leads to no positive resolution of the problems that abound in the world. Because of the confusion associated with pacifism and passivity, John Dear and other notable peace seekers such as Mohandas Gandhi and Martin Luther King, Jr., have preferred the term "active nonviolence."

—Patricia Patten Normile, S.F.O., *John Dear on Peace: An Introduction to His Life and Works*

### Questions for Reflection

*Do you think of pacifists as "passive" individuals, content to let the world order to proceed as it is?*

*Do you believe you can be patriotic and not support certain wars? How do you feel about your country's current policies concerning foreign wars? Are you even aware of its current policies on war? What do you agree with or disagree with?*

## Active Nonviolence as Energy and Creativity

Active nonviolence is full of the energy of life and the creativity of humankind. It exudes a fervent desire for a better world. Active nonviolence searches, prays and works for alternatives to passivity or the destructive hatred that arises from injustice and violence.... Active nonviolence...seeks ways to address the crisis situation through positive activity. Active nonviolence strives to defuse violence and certainly not to create additional hostile acts in response to a crisis. Retaliation cannot coexist with active nonviolence.

—Patricia Patten Normile, s.f.o., *John Dear on Peace: An Introduction to His Life and Works*

## Questions for Reflection

*Do you have a "fervent desire for a better world"? What are your hopes for this world?*

*Do you search, pray, and work for alternatives to passivity or the destructive hatred that arises from injustice and violence?*

## What Is Peace?

What is peace? Is it just a state of nonviolence? We tend to think of it as a state of inaction, placidness. We think of it as an inactive space, such as calm water. But what if peace is a force, a quiet force but a powerful one? What if this force is capable of inciting a "riot" of more peace? What if the force of peace is greater than the force of war? Gandhi understood this in our age—and Saint Francis understood this in his age.... These powerful instances of witnessing changed lives, just as surely as swords and bombs.

—Susan Saint Sing, *Francis and the San Damiano Cross:*
*Meditations on Spiritual Transformation*

## Questions for Reflection

*Do you see peace as a "force"?*

*Has there ever been a time when the force of peace was greater than the force of war? When? Was it in your lifetime?*

## Peace at Home First

If the lilies of peace are to thrive in the world, they must first flourish in our families.

—Gloria Hutchinson, *Praying the Rosary*

## Questions for Reflection

*How can peace in the world be possible if there isn't even peace among people in their own families? Imagine a current family battle that is being waged. Why is it so difficult to get the two parties to agree or compromise? What is getting in the way of their peace and love for one another? Now imagine two world leaders, who are not related and have no mutual or shared past or loving relationship. Can you understand why it is so difficult for them to get along? How can we expect our world leaders to behave peacefully and get along, when we can't even do so at home with the people we love the most?*

## Praying the Rosary for Peace

And the rosary is by nature a family prayer in which the church joins the Blessed Mother in focusing on her Son. We pray with her and through her intercession, certain of her maternal regard for all that concerns us. As John Paul II points out, praying the rosary in families and for families is a life-giving experience. "Individual family members, in turning their eyes towards Jesus," he writes, "also regain the ability to look one another in the eye to communicate, to show solidarity, to forgive one another, and to see their covenant of love renewed in the Spirit of God" (*RVM*, #41).

—Gloria Hutchinson, *Praying the Rosary*

## Questions for Reflection

*When was the last time you prayed the rosary? How important is praying the rosary to your daily life?*

*Pray the rosary daily for a week. Offer it up for world peace, keeping the world's children especially in mind. How does it make you feel? Do you feel more hopeful about the world?*

# Notes

. . . . .

*The following books were all published by St. Anthony Messenger Press, Cincinnati, Ohio.*

## For Every Matter Under Heaven

p. 2.   Beth M. Knobbe, *Finding My Voice: A Young Woman's Perspective*, pp. 46–47.

p. 3.   Knobbe, p. 47.

p. 4.   Mary H. Reaman, *Wake Up to God's Word: Exercises for Spiritual Transformation*, p. 29.

p. 5.   Reaman, p. 29.

p. 6.   Knobbe, pp. 15, 16.

p. 7.   Ilia Delio, O.S.F., *The Humility of God: A Franciscan Perspective*, p. 156.

## A Time to Be Born

p. 9.   Ginny Kubitz Moyer, *Mary and Me: Catholic Women Reflect on the Mother of God*, p. 8.

p. 10.  Moyer, p. 11.

p. 11.  Clare Wagner, *Awakening to Prayer: A Woman's Perspective*, p. 74.

p. 12.  Wagner, p. 75.

p. 13.  Tammy Bundy, *The Book of Mom: What Parents Know By Heart*, pp. 151–152.

p. 14.  Bundy, p. 127.

## A Time to Die

p. 16.  Dolores R. Leckey, *Grieving With Grace: A Woman's Perspective*, p. xv.

p. 17.  Leckey, p. 18.

p. 18.  Lyn Holley Doucet, *Healing Troubled Hearts: Daily Spiritual Exercises*, p. 142.

p. 19.  Janice McGrane, S.S.J., *Saints to Lean On: Spiritual Companions for Illness and Disability*, p. x.

p. 20.  Gloria Hutchinson, *Be Comforted: Healing in Times of Loss, Anger, Anxiety, Loneliness, Sickness, Death*, p. 109.

p. 21.  Hutchinson, p. 110.

## A Time to Plant, A Time to Pluck Up What Is Planted

p. 23.  Pegge Bernecker, *Your Spiritual Garden: Tending to the Presence of God*, p. 124.

p. 24.  Bernecker, p. 124.

p. 25.  Bernecker, p. 124.

p. 26.  Judith Dunlap, *Bringing Home the Gospel: The Year of Matthew*, p. 72.

p. 27.  Reaman, p. 29.

p. 28.  Reaman, p. 31.

## A Time to Kill, A Time to Heal

p. 31.  Michelle A. Gonzalez, *Embracing Latina Spirituality: A Woman's Perspective*, p. 70.

p. 32.  Doucet, p. 159.

p. 33.  Wagner, pp. 79–80.

p. 34.  Wagner, p. 79.

p. 35.  Leckey, p. 18.

p. 36.  Maryanne Raphael, *What Mother Teresa Taught Me*, p. 197.

## A Time to Break Down, A Time to Build Up

p. 38.  Joan Mueller, *Living a Spirituality of Action: A Woman's Perspective*, p. 29.

p. 39.  Susan K. Rowland, *Make Room for God: Clearing Out the Clutter*, pp. 11–12.

p. 40.  Joanne Turpin, *Women in Church History: 21 Stories for 21 Centuries*, p. 122.

p. 41.  Elizabeth Bookser Barkley, *Woman to Woman: Seeing God in Daily Life*, p. 13.

p. 42.  Barkley, p. 17.

p. 43.  Barkley, p. 28.

p. 44.  Susan K. Rowland, *Healing After Divorce: Hope for Catholics*, p. 98

## A Time to Weep, A Time to Laugh

p. 47.  Mueller, p. 20.

p. 48.  Carol Luebering, *Coping With Loss: Praying Your Way to Acceptance*, pp. 19–20.

p. 49.  Leckey, p. 31.

p. 50.  Ilia Delio, O.S.F.., Keith Douglass Warner, O.F.M., and Pamela Wood, *Care for Creation: A Franciscan Spirituality of the Earth*, pp. 78.

p. 51.  Bernecker, p. 127.

p. 52.  Hutchinson, p. 51.

p. 53.  Hutchinson, p. 51

## A Time to Mourn, A Time to Dance

p. 56.  Susan Saint Sing, *Spirituality of Sport: Balancing Body and Soul*, p. 13.

p. 57.  Saint Sing, *Spirituality of Sport*, p. 14.

p. 58.  Saint Sing, *Spirituality of Sport*, p. 14.

p. 59.  Elizabeth A. Dreyer, *Making Sense of God: A Woman's Perspective*, p. 69.

p. 60.  Dreyer, p. 69.

p. 61. Rowland, *Healing After Divorce*, p. 78.

p. 62. Sidney Callahan, *Creating New Life, Nurturing Families: A Woman's Perspective*, p. 39.

## A Time to Throw Away Stones, A Time to Gather Stones Together

p. 65. Susan K. Rowland, *Make Room for God: Clearing Out the Clutter*, pp. 42–43.

p. 66. Rowland, *Make Room for God*, p. 91.

p. 67. Rowland, *Make Room for God*, p. 25.

p. 68. Delio, et al., *Care for Creation*, pp. 161–162.

p. 69. Ilia Delio, O.S.F., *Clare of Assisi: A Heart Full of Love*, p. 12.

p. 70. Delio, et al., *Care for Creation*, p. 59.

## A Time to Embrace, A Time to Refrain From Embracing

p. 73. Moyer, p. 25.

p. 74. Moyer, p. 31.

p. 75. Rowland, *Healing After Divorce*, p. 6.

p. 76. Rowland, *Healing After Divorce*, p. 10.

p. 77. Dreyer, p. 78.

p. 78. Patricia Cooney Hathaway, *Weaving Faith and Experience: A Woman's Perspective*, p. 28.

p. 79. Wagner, p. 75.

## A Time to Seek, A Time to Lose

p. 81. Bernecker, p. 126.

p. 82. Carol Luebering, *Coping With Loss: Praying Your Way to Acceptance*, p. ix.

p. 83. Knobbe, p. 42.

p. 84. Knobbe, p. 42.

p. 85. Luebering, p. xii.

p. 86. Cooney Hathaway, p. 29.

**A Time to Keep, A Time to Throw Away**

p. 89. Wagner, p. 20.

p. 90. Wagner, p. 21.

p. 91. Delio, *Clare of Assisi: A Heart Full of Love*, p. 29.

p. 92. Delio, *Clare of Assisi*, p. 29.

p. 93. Mueller, p. 29.

p. 94. Delio, *Clare of Assisi*, p. 29.

p. 95. Rowland, *Make Room for God*, p. 33.

**A Time to Tear, A Time to Sew**

p. 98. Mueller, p. 36.

p. 99. Mueller, p. 36.

p. 100. Cooney Hathaway, p. 19.

p. 101. Cooney Hathaway, pp. 19–20.

p. 102. Cooney Hathaway, p. 29.

**A Time to Keep Silence, A Time to Speak**

p. 105. Dreyer, p. 77.

p. 106. Doucet, p. 24.

p. 107. Doucet, p. 25

p. 108. Dunlap, p. 99.

p. 109. Leckey, p. 18.

## A Time to Love, A Time to Hate

p. 112. Callahan, p. 13.

p. 113. Callahan, p. 15.

p. 114. Callahan, p. 48.

p. 115. Callahan, p. 48.

p. 116. Donna Erickson Couch, *Together But Alone: When God Means Something Different to Your Spouse*, pp. 61–62.

p. 117. Raphael, p. 191.

p. 118. Couch, pp. 108–109.

## A Time for War, A Time for Peace

p. 121. Patricia Patten Normile, S.F.O., *John Dear on Peace: An Introduction to His Life and Works*, p. 59.

p. 122. Normile, p. 60.

p. 123. Normile, p. 60.

p. 124. Saint Sing, *Francis and the San Damiano Cross*, p. x.

p. 125. Gloria Hutchinson, *Praying the Rosary*, p. 5.